RATIONAL FASTING

...for...

Physical, Mental and Spiritual Rejuvenation

By ARNOLD EHRET

also

Health and Happiness Through Fasting

By FRED S. HIRSCH

Published by
EHRET LITERATURE PUBLISHING CO.

BEAUMONT, CALIFORNIA 92223

Ninth Edition

Copyright, © 1971
Ehret Literature Publishing Co.
Beaumont, California 92223
Printed in U.S.A.

Yours for "Ehretism"

Prof Arnold Ehret.

Foreword

by Fred S. Hirsch

IT'S EASY TO FAST

Many health teachers and disciples of fasting have long expounded this "wonder cure" — but it remained for Arnold Ehret, considered by many the greatest exponent of fasting, to give suffering humanity the complete knowledge of "how to conduct and complete" a successful fast.

There are many types of a Fast and most of them are more or less effective. But the TOTAL fast — NO food of any kind whatsoever — simply water as desired, is the most commonly practiced. A restricted diet of one kind of fruit alone such as grapes, watermelon, cherries, oranges, apples, etc. and the so-called "milk diet" are also often known as fasting. Dried fruits, with liquids of all kinds restricted, is a form of fasting known as the Schroth cure.

Above all else, the individual who has decided to take a fast must have the courage of his convictions. To know "how long one should fast" and especially "how to break a fast" is of utmost importance. Arnold Ehret was perhaps the first of the great health teachers to recognize that "Fasters who died from too long a fast actually suffocated in their own filth, and NOT from lack of food". The Faster must know what physical conditions change rapidly during a fast. "Waste" when in the circulation makes you feel miserable but as soon as it is eliminated you feel fine.

Longevity is a natural desire of all mankind — but only if one is free from aches and pains. Arnold Ehret now contributes the necessary knowledge which if followed will enable a long suffering humanity to enjoy the full life of a centenarian, mentally alert and physically virile. Even the dream of lasting youth and beauty is now about to become true.

Preface

Are you one of the thousands of present age persons — discouraged and disheartened on account of ill-health; is your faith in so-called cures shattered after having tried them without results; are you only able to use a small percent of the vitality that good Mother Nature endows her beloved ones with? Probably you have been told that only an operation will save you. Somehow, when we suffer organic trouble we fail to think clearly and permit ourselves to be easily persuaded into operations. If you are one of these unfortunates DON'T GIVE UP HOPE. For "he that hath health hath hope, and he that hath hope, hath everything."

"Since man degenerated through civilization, he no longer knows what to do when he becomes sick". The genuine principles of healing are simple and few. Our very lack of appetite which occurs when we are sick is Nature's method of teaching her children. One might properly call this a "forced fast". These are but a few of the truisms taught by Arnold Ehret in his many writings. Our greatest possession is health.

This Drugless Healing is not limited in its scope; and thru its proper application and use it restores normal functioning overcoming practically all ailments to which the human family is subject.

"TRUTH WEARS NO MASK; BOWS AT NO HUMAN SHRINE: SEEKS NEITHER PLACE NOR APPLAUSE: SHE ASKS ONLY A HEARING." — Redfield.

Contents

Frontispiece, ARNOLD EHRET

Part I

The Fundamental Cause in the Nature of Disease	9
Remedies for the Removal of Fundamental Causes and Prevention of Their Re-occurrence	26
The Fundamental Cause of Growing Old	31
The Preservation of the Hair	35
Increasing Longevity	40

Part II

Complete Instructions for Fasting	43
Rational Fasting for Physical, Mental and Spiritual Rejuvenation	44
Building a Perfect Body Thru Fasting	47
Important Rules for the Faster	51
Rules During Fast	53
Short Fasts and the Non-Breakfast Plan	56
Fasting for Spiritual Rebirth	60
Conclusion	62

Part III

Health & Happiness Thru Fasting	65
How Long Should One Fast	70
Why to Fast	71
When and How to Fast	73
Why to Fast	81
Where to Fast	82
How Long to Fast	83

The Common Fundamental Cause in the Nature of Diseases

All the phases of the process of development of the medical science including those of the earliest periods of civilization, have in their way of understanding the casual nature of diseases, that one thing in common i.e.: that the diseases, owing to external causes, enter into the human body and thus, by force of a necessary or at least unavoidable law, disturb the body in its existence, cause it pain and at last destroy it. Even modern medical science, no matter how scientifically enlightened it pretends to be, has not quite turned away from this basic note of demoniac interpretation. In fact, the most modern achievement, bacteriology, rejoices over every newly discovered bacillus as a further addition to the army of beings whose accepted task it is to endanger the life of man.

Looking at it from a philosophical standpoint, this interpretation differs from the mediaeval superstition and the period of fetishism only in the supplemental name. Formerly it was an "evil spirit," which imagination went so far as to believe in "satanic personages"; now this same dangerous monster is a microscopically visible being whose existence has been proven beyond any doubt.

The matter, it is true, has still a great drawback in the so-called "disposition" — a fine word! — But what we really are to understand by it, nobody has ever told us. All the tests on animals, with their symptom-reactions, do not prove anything sure, because these occur only by means of injection into the blood-circulation and never by introduction into the digestive channel through the mouth.

There is something true in the conception of "external invasion" of a disease, as well as in heredity, however not in the sense that the invader is a spirit (demon) hostile to life, or a microscopic being (bacillus); but all *diseases* without exception, even the hereditary, are caused — disregarding a few other hygienic causes — by biologically wrong, "unnatural" food and by each ounce of over-nourishment, only and exclusively.

First of all I maintain that in all diseases without exception there exists a tendency by the organism to secrete mucus, and in case of a more advanced stage — pus (decomposed blood). Of course every healthy organism must also contain a certain mucus — lymph, a fatty substance of the bowels, etc., of a mucus nature. Every expert will admit this in all catarrhalic cases, from a harmless cold in the nose to inflammation of the lungs and consumption, as well as in epilepsy (attacks showing froth at the mouth, mucus). Where this secretion of mucus does not show freely and openly, as in cases of ear, eye, skin or stomach trouble, heart diseases, rheumatism, gout, etc., even in all degrees of insanity, mucus is the main factor of the illness. The natural secretive-organs unable to cope with it longer, the mucus enters the blood causing heat, inflammation, pain and fever at the respective spot where the vessel-system is probably contracted owing to an over-cooling fever (cold), heat, inflammation, pain, fever, etc.

We need only to give a patient of any kind nothing but "mucusless" food, for instance; fruit or even nothing but water or lemonade; we then find that the entire digestive energy, freed for the first time, throws itself upon the mucus-matters, accumulated since childhood and frequently hardened, as well as on the "pathologic beds" formed therefrom. And the result? With unconditional certainty this mucus which I mark as the common basic and main cause of all diseases will appear in the urine and in the excrements. If the disease is already somewhat advanced so that in some spot, even in the innermost interior, there have appeared pathologic beds, i.e., decomposed cellular tissues, then pus is also being secreted. As soon as the introduction of mucus by means of "artificial food," fat meat, bread, potatoes, farinaceous products, rice, milk, etc., ceases, the blood-circulation attacks the mucus and the pus of the body themselves and secretes them through the urine, and in the case of heavily infected bodies, even through all the openings at their command as well as through the mucus membranes.

If potatoes, grain-meal, rice or the respective meat-materials are boiled long enough, we receive jelly-like slime (mucus) or paste used by bookbinders and carpenters. This mucus substance soon becomes sour, ferments, and forms a bed for fungi, moulds and bacilli. In the digestion, which is nothing else but a boiling, a combustion, this slime or paste is being secreted in the same manner, for the blood can use only the exdigested sugar transformed from starch. The secreted matter, the superfluous product, i.e., this paste or slime is being completely excreted in the beginning. It is, therefore, easy to understand that in the course of life the intestines and the stomach are gradually being pasted and slimed up to such an extent that this paste of floral and this slime of faunal origin turn into fermentation, clog up the blood-vessels and finally decompose the stagnated blood. If figs, dates or grapes are boiled down thick enough we also receive a pap which, however, does not turn to fermentation and never secretes slime, but which is called syrup. Fruit-sugar, the most important thing for the blood, is also sticky, it is true, but is being completely used up by the body as the highest form of fuel, and leaves for excretion only traces of cellulose, which, not being sticky, is promptly excreted and does not ferment. Boiled-down sugar, owing to its resistance against fermentation, is even used for the preservation of food.

Each healthy or sick person deposits on the tongue a sticky mucus as soon as he reduces his food or fasts. This occurs also on the mucus membrane of the stomach, of which the tongue is an exact copy. In the first stool after fasting this mucus makes its appearance.

I recommend to my reader or to the physicians and searchers to test my claims by way of experiments which alone are entitled to real scientific recognition. The experiment, the question put to nature, is the basis of a natural science and reveals the infallible truth, no matter whether it is stated by me or somebody else. Furthermore, I recommend the following experiments to those who are brave enough to test on their own bodies which I undertook on mine. They will receive the same answer from nature, i.e., from their organism, provided that the latter be sound in my sense. "Exact" to a certain degree reacts only to the clean, sound, mucusless organism. After a two years' strict fruit-diet with intercalated fasting cures, I had attained a degree of health which is simply not imaginable nowadays and which allowed of my making the following experiments:

With a knife I made an incision in my lower arm; there was no flow of blood as it thickened instantly; closing up the wound, no inflammation, no pain, no mucus and pus:

healed up in three days, blood crust thrown off. Later, with vegetaric food, including mucus-ferments (starch food), but without eggs and milk: The wound bled a little, caused some pain and pussed slightly, a light inflammation, complete healing only after some time. After that the same wounding, with meat-food and some alcohol: longer bleeding, the blood of a light color, red and thin, inflammation, pain, pussing for several days, and healing only after a two days' fasting.

I have offered myself, of course in vain, to the Prussian Ministry of War for a repetition of this experiment. Why is it that the wounds of the Japanese healed much quicker and better in the Russo-Japanese war than those of the "Meat and Brandy Russians"? Has nobody for 2,000 years ever thought it over why the opening of the artery and even the poison cup could not kill Seneca, after he had despised meat and fasted in prison? It is said that even before that, Seneca fed on nothing but fruit and water.

All disease is finally nothing else but a clogging up of the smallest blood vessels, the capillaries, by mucus. Nobody will want to clean the water conduit of a city, a pipe system, which is fed with soiled water by a pump, the filters of which are clogged up, without having the water-supply shut off during the cleaning process. If the conduit supplies the entire city or a portion of it with unclean water, or if even the smallest branch-pipes are clogged up, there is no man in the world who would repair or improve that respective spot; everybody thinks at once of the central, of the tank and the filters, and these together with the pumping machine can be cleaned only as long as the water supply is shut off.

"I am the Lord, thy physician" — English and modern: nature alone heals, cleans, "unmucuses" best and infallibly sure, but only if the supply, or at least the mucus supply, is stopped. Each "physiological machine," man like beast, cleanses itself immediately, dissolves the mucus in the clogged-up vessels, without stopping short as soon as the supply of compact food at least, is interrupted. Even in the case of the supposedly healthy man this mucus, as already mentioned then appears in the urine where it can be seen after cooling off in the proper glass tubes! Whoever denies, ignores or fights this uniform fact, because perhaps, it is not in accord with his teachings, or is not sufficiently scientific, is jointly guilty of the impossibility of detection of the principal cause of all diseases.

Therewith I also uncover the last secret of consumption. Or does anybody believe that this enormous quantity of mucus thrown off by a patient stricken with tuberculosis for years and years emanates only from the lung itself? Just because this patient is then almost forcibly fed on "mucus" (pap, milk, fat meats) the mucus can never cease until the lung itself decays and the "bacilli" make the appearance when death becomes inevitable. The mystery of the bacilli is solved simply thus: The gradual clogging up of the blood vessels by mucus leads to decomposition, to fermentation of these mucus products and "boiled-dead" food residues. These decay partially on the living body (pussy abcesses, cancer, tuberculosis, syphilis, lupus, etc.). Now everybody knows that meat, cheese and all organic matter will again "germinate, put forth bacilli" during the process of decomposition. It is for this reason that these germs appear and are detectable only in the more advanced stage of the disease, when, however, they are not the cause but the product of the disease, and disease-furthering only in so far as the decomposition, for instance, of the lung, is being hastened by them, because the excretion of the bacilli, their toxines, act poisoning. If it be correct that bacilli invade, "infect" from the exterior, then it is nothing but the mucus which makes possible their activity, and furnishes the proper soil; the "disposition."

As already stated, I have repeatedly (once for two years) lived mucusless, i.e., on fruit exclusively. I was no longer in need of a handkerchief which product of civilization I hardly need even up to this date. Has anyone ever seen a healthy animal living in freedom, expectorate or blow its nose? A chronic inflammation of the kidneys, considered deadly, which I was stricken with, was not only healed, but I am enjoying a degree of health and efficiency which by far surpasses even that of my healthiest youth. I want to see the man who, being sick unto death at 31; who can run for two hours and a quarter without a stop, or make an endurance march of 56 hours' duration — eight years later.

It is surely theoretically correct that man was a mere fruit eater in times gone by, and biologically correct, that he can be it even today. Or can the horse-sense of man not conceive without any direct proofs, of the fact that man, before becoming a hunter, lived on fruits only? I even maintain that he did live in absolute health, beauty and strength without pain and grief just the way the Bible says. Fruit only, the sole "mucusless" food, is natural. Everything prepared by man, or supposedly improved by him, is evil. The arguments regarding fruit are scientifically exact; in the apple or banana, for instance, everything can be found contained what man needs. Man is so perfect that he can live on one kind of fruit only, at least for quite some time. This has been conclusively proven by the Mono-diet system of August Engelhardt who solved by his great philosophy and practice of natural life all problems of mankind. But a self-evident truth preached by nature must not be discarded just because no one has been able to apply it in actual practice on account of civilizational considerations. From the eating of fruit only one gets first a crisis, i.e., cleansing. No man would have ever believed me, that it is possible to live without food for 126 days, in which 49 were undertaken at a stretch, during a period covering 14 months. Now I have done it, and yet this truth is not being understood. Hitherto I state and will teach only this fact, that fruit is the most natural "healing remedy." Whether my calculation is correct will be proven by the next epidemic. I take, however this opportunity to uncover the reasons why the self-evident is not believed in. When in the previous century someone talked about the possibility of phoning from London to Paris, everybody laughed because there had never been such a thing. Natural food is not being believed in any more, because almost no one practices it and living in to-day's civilization, we cannot easily practice it. It must also be considered that contra-interests fear that the prices of other, artificial foodstuffs may drop, and others fear that the food-physiology may receive a shock and physicians become unnecessary. But it is just this fasting and fruit cure which requires very strict observation and instruction — therefore: more doctors and less patients who, however, will gladly pay more if they get well. Thus, the social question regarding doctors is solved — an assertion already made by me publicly in Zurich several years ago.

Almost all fasting attempts fail through ignorance of the fact that with the beginning of the mucusless diet the old mucus is being excreted so much more forcibly until that person is absolutely clean and healthy. THUS THE SEEMINGLY HEALTHY PERSON HAS FIRST TO PASS THROUGH A CONDITION OF SICKNESS (CLEANSING), or go through an intermediate stage of illness to a higher level of health.

This is the "great-cliff" around which so few Vegetarians have failed to go — discarding the basic truth just like the mass of people are doing. I have proven this fact in the "Vegetarische Warte" completely on the basis of experiments and facts; and refuting their greatest objection, that of undernourishment, by an actual fasting experiment of 49 days; with a preceding fruit diet. My state of health was greatly improved thru this radical excretion of mucus, disregarding a few unhygienic circumstances during the test. I received numerous letters of appreciation, especially from the educated classes. The mass of adherents of vegetarianism "mucuses" gaily ahead. Contrasting herewith it can only be said that the poisons (so-called by them): meat, alcohol, coffee and tobacco are in the long run comparatively harmless, AS LONG AS THEY ARE USED MODERATELY.

In order to avoid misunderstanding on the part of teetotalers and vegetarians, I must insert here a few explanations. Meat is not a foodstuff but only a stimulant which ferments, decays in the stomach, the process of decay, however, does not begin in the stomach, but at once after the slaughtering. This has already been proven on living persons by Prof. Dr. S. Graham, and I complete this fact by saying that meat acts as a stimulant just by means of these poisons of decay, and therefore is being erroneously regarded as a strengthening foodstuff. Or is there anyone who can show me chemico-physiologically that the albumen molecule going through the process of decay is being newly reformed in the stomach and celebrates its resurrection in some muscle of the human body? Like alcohol, the meat produces in the beginning stimulating strength and energy until the entire organism is penetrated by it and the break-down inevitable. All the other stimulants act likewise. This, therefore, is a false delusion.

The fundamental evil of all non-vegetaric forms of diet consist always in the overeating of meat, as it is the origin of all the other evils, especially in the craving af alhocol. If fruit is eaten almost exclusively, the eagerness for cup or glass loses itself to chastise himself against it, simply because meat produces the demon thirst. Alcohol is a proven kind of antidote for meat, and the gourmand of the big city, who eats practically nothing but meat, must therefore have wines, Mocha and Havana, in order to at least in some way counteract the heavy meat-poisoning. It is a well-known fact, that, after an opulent dinner, one feels decidedly fresher, physically and mentally, if the stimulants, poisonous in themselves, are taken moderately rather than to stuff one's self full with the "good-eating" to the very fatigue.

I ABSOLUTELY DECLARE WAR ON MEAT AND ALCOHOL; through fruit and moderate eating these great evils are radically diminished. But whoever finds it impossible to entirely give up meat and alcohol is, if he takes them moderately, still far ahead of the vegetaric eater. The American, Fletcher proved this most evidently by his tremendous success, and his secret is explained by my experiments which show that a person becomes most efficient and develops best in health if he eats as little as possible. Are not the oldest people as a rule the poorest? Have not the greatest discoverers and inventors sprung from poverty, i.e., been little eaters? Were not the greatest of mankind, the prophets, founders of religions, etc. ascetics? Is that culture, to dine excellently thrice a day, and is it social progress that each working man eats five times a day and then pumps himself full with beer at night? If the sick organism can regenerate by eating nothing, I think the logical consequence is that a healthy organism needs but little food in order to remain healthy, strong and persevering.

All so-called miracles of the saints have their only origin in ascetics, and are today impossible for the sole reason that, although much praying is done, no fasting is adhered to. This is the only solution of this quarrel. We have no more miracles because we have no more saints, i.e., sanctified and healed by ascetics and fastings. The saints were self-shining, expressed in modern language: medial or radioactive, but only because through asceticism, they were "godly" healthy, and not "by special grace." I just wish to mention here that I myself have succeeded in visible, electric effluences, but only by external and internal sun-energies (sun-baths and food from the "sun-kitchen," fruit).

The entire world is quarreling now regarding these questions and miracles. And here is the solution on the basis of experiments which everybody can repeat if he is brave enough. But it is apparently easier to write books, preach and pray, or to say that I am an exception. This is true, but only so far as pluck and understanding are concerned. Physiologically all men are equal, and whoever cannot be moderate may learn it from me if he wishes to be a real searcher after health.

If a man eats little and is healthy he can, for quite a length of time, digest the most absurd food, meat and starch (mucus), i.e., he can excrete it naturally. He becomes and remains still more perfect and clean if he eats but little fruit, and of this he needs the least because it is the most perfect food. This eternal truth by natural law, man of today will and cannot admit, and has a well-founded fear of it, because he is built up of dead-boiled food and his cells die off and are excreted as soon as he takes his sunbaths, fasts or eats the living cells of fruit. But this cure must be done with the greatest care. The duty of medicine is to protect man from a breakdown of his cells, to hold him above water as long as this is possible only to cause him to die of the disease so much more promptly and quickly which today is fervently wished for. Vegetarianism cannot deny that the consumers of meat and alcohol can also boast of much health and great deeds and high age but taken individually and as a people only so long as but little is eaten and no over-nourishment caused. Eating "too much" takes less revenge in case of meat-eating because meat contains proportionally less "mucus" than starch containing, "mucus" vegetaric food and the celebrated vegetaric dinners with entirely too many dishes daily. I myself have not cared for many years for any meals; I eat only when I have appetite and then so little that it does not cause any harmful effect, if, on account of an experiment, I am obliged to eat something which in itself is not entirely free from objection.

If the most serious diseases can be cured by fasting—which has been proven in thousands of cases—and if during the fast one becomes stronger "if it is done right," then the most energetic food, the fruit, should cause one so much the more to become strong and healthy. This has also been scientifically proven by the merited Dr. Bircher. It is true, the science of cure by nature has recognized the fact that something must get out of the sick organism, but it has so far ascribed the greatest importance to physical stimulations ignoring completely the real natural moment to the process of cure; the abstaining from food and thru following a fruit-diet. At least, they have only offered a substitute by a non-alcohol and meatless diet. This does not mean much in the face of my "mucus-theory." And what is this mucusless alcohol not accused of today? It will soon be made the "scape-goat" of all diseases, because here and there is found a depraved one who, consuming it in enormous quantities, ends in delirium. Just compel a drinker to fast a few days or to eat nothing but fruit—I will wager that the best glass of beer will have lost its flavor for him. This proves that the entire "civilized" mess, from beefsteak down to apparently harmless oatmeals, creates the desire for these detested antidotes: alcohol, coffee, tea, tobacco. Why? **Because much-eating paralyzes and only the use of stimulants restores!**

Here is the true and fundamental reason for the increase of alcohol consumption: the over-nourishment, especially with meat. Prof. Dr. Graham says in his "Physiology of Nourishment": "A drinker can reach a high age, a glutton never." This is true, because the acute alcohol acts as a stimulant, especially the modern beer, is less harmful in the long run than the chronic stuffing up of the digestive channel with mucus food.

I now ask: what appeals more to reason—to wipe out the masses of mucus, piled up since childhood, or having infected

—21—

the cellular tissues of the body by poisonous Drugs, or parts cut away by useless, avoidable operations; having the cure delayed by one-sided Osteopathy; Chiropractic fanaticism; misunderstood Electric methods, mucus forming and unclean milk cures, weakening Hot Springs treatments; the Christian Science superstition, etc., or simply to stop the further supply of mucus caused by unnatural Diet? Or is there anybody who would like to prove to me that the most skillful Chef or Confectioner is capable of producing something better than an apple, a grape or banana? If nourishment by mucus and over-eating is the true fundamental cause of all diseases without exception, which I can prove to anybody on his own body, then there can exist but one natural remedy, i.e., fasting and fruit-diet. That every animal fasts in case of even the slightest uneasiness, is a well-known fact and to culture and thanks to man feeding them, domestic animals have lost their sharp instinct for the right kind of food and the natural hours of feeding—and therewith their proper state of health and acuteness of sense—they will never-the-less when sick, accept only the most necessary food; they fast themselves back to health. Poor, sick man, however, must under no circumstances live on short rations for more than 1 or 2 days, for fear that he may "lose strength."

Already many leading physicians have called fasting: wonder cures, cure of the uncured, cure of all cures, etc. Certain charlatans have brought this infallible, **but at the same time, dangerous cure,** to discredit. I have done in fasting the most significant thing in centuries: 49 days, world-record (see "Vegetarsche Warte," 1909, book 19, 20, 22, 1920, book 1 and 2). Furthermore I am the only one who combines this cure with systematically and individually adapted fruit diet, which makes it astonishingly easier and absolutely harmless. We are, therefore, undoubtedly put in a position to heal diseases which the school of medicine designates as incurable. On the basis of my deduction that this mucus coming from cultured food, is the fundamental cause and main factor in the nature of all diseases, symptoms of age, obesity, falling out of the hair, wrinkles, weakness of nerves and memory, etc., there is justified hope for the creation of a new phase of development of the progressive healing methods and biological medicine.

Already Hippokrates had uniformly recognized the "disease-material" for all diseases. Prof. Jager has defined the "Common" as "Stench," but has not discovered the source of this "bad smell." Dr. Lahmann and other representatives of the physical dietetic tendency, especially Kuhne, came on to the tracks of the "common foreign matter." But not one of them showed, recognized or proved by experiment, that it is this very mucus of culture-food which loads up our organism from childhood, and attacks it at a certain degree of fermentation, forms pathologic beds, i.e., decomposes the cellular tissue of the body itself into pus and decay. It is being mobilized in case of casual colds or high temperatures, etc., and produces, in its tendency to leave the body, symptoms of abnormal functions which hitherto have been regarded as the disease itself. It is, therefore, for the first time possible to define what is meant by "decomposition." The more the "mucus" (bad mother's milk and all its substitutes) is being administered from childhood on, or the less this mucus is being excreted, owing to hereditary weakness, through the organs made to perform this task, the greater is the inclination to catch cold, fever, to freeze, to admit parasites, to get sick and to pre-maturely grow old. Very likely by this the veil has been lifted from the secret which hitherto has always surrounded the nature of the white corpuscles. I believe that here, as in many other cases, we are confronted with an error of medical science. The bacteria throw themselves upon the white corpuscles, composed to the largest extent of this mucus; denounced by me. Are not the bacteria being bred on this mucus by the millions outside of the organism?—on potatoes, broth, gelatine, i.e., on mucus, i.e., nitrogenous, vegetable or animal substances consisting of an alkalically reacting fluid containing granulated cells of the appearance of the white blood-corpuscles? Perhaps in an entirely healthy condition the so-called mucus membrane should not at all be white, slimy, but clean and red like on animals. Perhaps this "corpse-mucus" is even the cause of the paleness of the white race! Paleface! Corpsecolor!

With this "mucus-theory" to be confirmed by experiment the spectre "disease" has been finally deprived of its demoniac mask. He who believes me can heal not only himself, if everything else fails, but we have for the first time been given the means to radically prevent disease and to make it definitely impossible. Even the dream of lasting youth and beauty is now about to become true.

The animal, and especially the human organism, is, from a mechanical standpoint, a complicated tube-system of blood-vessels with air-gas impetus by means of the lungs in which the blood-fluid is constantly kept moving and regulated by the heart as a valve. The decomposition of the air-gas is accomplished by each breath in the lungs (separating of the air into oxygen and nitrogen): thus the blood is constantly kept moving and the human body does its service incredibly long without fatigue. Let nobody come to me with the silly excuse of the "daily experience of the absolutely natural compulsion of much-eating," prescribed for working man, etc., before it has not been experienced by such complainant, how long it is possible to work or march, without fatigue, after fasting or fruit-food. Fatigue is in the first place a reducing of strength by too much digestion-work, secondly a clogging-up of the heated and consequently narrowed-down blood-vessels, and thirdly a "self-and re-poisoning" through the excretion of mucus during the motion. All organic substances of animal origin excrete cyanate groupes in their decomposition, which the chemist Hensel has defined as bacilli proper. The air is not only the highest and most perfect operating material of the human body, but simultaneously the first element for the erection, repair, substitute, and very likely, the animal organism derives nitrogen also from the air. On certain caterpillars an increase of weight through air alone has been stated.

Remedies for the Removal of the Common Fundamental Cause of Diseases and the Prevention of Their Re-occurrence

After having told my readers the dread and horror of being sick or getting sick, in the previous chapter, it befits me to show them the means and ways, as far as this, commonly speaking, is possible, how to successfully encounter mucus-poisoning, this greatest foe of health. Here I wish to show three means and ways which can produce a beneficial change.

1. The shortest and best way is the fasting so much talked about in this book. It cuts short the life of the "grim misdoer" in our body and causes him to flee, and he leaves us faster with fright and terror.

Healthy people can submit themselves to a fasting cure without any further ceremony. It goes without saying that they must fast reasonably and assume personal responsibility, and not cause dangerous over-exertions during the fasting period, by demanding of themselves physical or mental performances which they could not live up to even at full fare. I insert here a precautionary measure which must be observed in all fasting cures; the complete emptying of the bowels at the beginning of the fasting by harmless purgative (such as an aromatic herb compound), or by a syringe, or by both. It lies in the nature of the thing that he who fasts must not be bothered by gas or decomposing matter which form from the excrements remaining in the bowels; it suffices that the mucus during the excretion gives him enough trouble, as already stated.

If it is not desired to take a more prolonged fast, although he is healthy, one should try a short one. Even a fasting of thirty-six hours, weekly one or two times, can be depended upon to produce very favorable results. It is best to start by leaving off the supper and taking an enema instead.

Then, in the case of a thirty-six hours' fast, nothing is eaten until the following morning, the meal to consist of nothing but fruits. The eating of fruit is desirable after each fasting, as the juices of the fruits cause a moving of the mucus-masses, which have loosened. However let me caution all; especially the sick and elderly people; this treatment must be carefully individualized.

One arrives at this result much sooner, however, if a longer fasting is done in the way described, for instance, three days, and then continue what I call an after-fasting cure. That is, do not eat anything for three days and drink only fresh lemonade, unsugared, in single gulps as may become necessary, and begin on the fourth day with some fruits. At the close of the fourth day take a thorough enema. More fruit may be added from day to day, until about the seventh day of the "after-cure" the normal quantity of fruit-diet in the proper composition and selection has been reached. The fasting, however, can be extended for weeks by healthy persons and by those whose occupation permits of their spending their time in bed in case of difficult excretions of mucus. Nobody should seriously object to the so-called "bad looks" or the decrease in weight. The body fasts itself into health, despite the miserable complexion, and in a remarkably short time the cheeks will be adorned by a healthy, natural red. The weight is also restored to its normal standard very soon after the fasting. After a fast the body reacts on every ounce of food. Very moderate eaters and frequently fasting people have a very fine, spiritual expression of the face. It is said that Pope Leo XIII, that great faster and life-artist, had a very clear, almost transparent complexion.

In this connection I wish to call attention to another point, already mentioned elsewhere, for the success of the fasting depends upon it to a great extent. **The fasting person must not unnecessarily become depressed or ill-humored;** the one condition finds relief in the disagreeable moments by complete rest, the other by quick and decided work, especially in light and mechanical occupation.

When the body has been ridden of the mucus, slime and paste, then it is the sacred duty of the person who has regained health to keep up the reclaimed highest earthly happiness and to guard it by means of natural, correct food. On this subject a few short remarks in the following paragraphs will not come amiss.

2. He who cannot fast, because of considerations of advanced lung or heart trouble, for instance, may at least see to it that the further accumulation of mucus be cut short by refraining from pronounced mucus-formers, especially from all flour (cake), rice, potato dishes, boiled milk, cheese, meat, etc. Whoever cannot miss bread entirely, must eat black or white bread only toasted; by toasting, the bread loses much of its harmfulness, as the mucus substances are partly destroyed. The eating of toasted bread or whole wheat Zweiback has the further advantage that not much can be eaten of it; it cannot be devoured as wild beasts do, and the necessary chewing

will fatigue even the most greedy gums. Whoever cannot bite the toasted bread, on account of bad teeth, may suck on it until it dissolves—a splendid way to restore declined strength. Whoever cannot miss potatoes should eat them only baked, and be sure and eat the jackets.

What then remains for "nutritious food" after I am to give up all albuminous food, like dried peas, lentils, beans, as much as possible? Thus many a reader will ask with a sigh.

As to the value of meat I have set forth my views elsewhere. The slight requirements in albumen are fully covered by sugary fruits; the banana, the nuts, combined with a few figs or dates are first class muscle-formers and strength-givers.

The vegetable (cut small and made into salad), the salads themselves, prepared with oil and plenty of lemon, and all the splendid fruits and berries, including those of the South, are worthy of being served on the tables of the gods. And when springtime comes, and last season's fruits, especially apples are on the decline, and the new vegetables not yet ready, does not Mother Nature help us out abundantly with oranges from the South? Will the aroma and wealth of these splendid products of nature not induce man to eventually become a fruit-eater entirely?

It is not possible for me to go into the question of food and its effects exhaustively in this book; for healthy people these statements may suffice, to sick people I recommend special prescriptions according to their state of health. If you are not already an owner of my Mucusless Diet Healing System Lesson Course may I suggest that you secure a copy of this book. (See list of other publications by Arnold Ehret, page 86.) It may be mentioned that non-fasters and people easily succumbing to illness, may at least follow the morning's fastings, or non-breakfast plan. It would be better for all concerned not to eat anything before 10 o'clock AM and then nothing but fruits. The reward for this little self-chastising will certainly show itself shortly—especially if the latter be kept up unfailingly.

3. Now, just one more word to those who think it impossible to give up the accustomed mucus food (meat, bread, etc.). To those "unfortunate ones" I give this advice: Chew your food, and each bite, thoroughly, as recommended by the American, Fletcher; in one word, "Fletcherize." Not that the fruit eaters should over-look this; but certainly the poison-laden "mucus-eaters" must do so; especially if they do not wish to sink into their graves all too soon.

The strong secretion of saliva in slow chewing decreases the formation of mucus and helps to prevent overeating. Of course, this group of individuals cannot expect to achieve in health and strength; retain youth and perseverance; physical and mental efficiency, as achieved by the faster and fruit-eater! Once man is healthy in my sense of the word, thru fasting and fruit diet; that is, free from mucus, slime and germs, and if he continues on the fruit-diet, he, of course, need not fast any longer; for only then will he find pleasure in eating which he never dreamt of before. Only in this way will man find the way to happiness, harmony and the solution of all health problems. Only through following this diet can man become want-free and get "nearest to divinity."

The Fundamental Cause of Growing Old and Ugly

THE MEANS FOUNDED IN NATURE FOR MAINTENANCE OF YOUTH AND BEAUTY

Following the previous general arguments to the effect that mucus is the main cause of disease and ageing, there is only left to show in particular and on the various organs, in how far the mucus of culture-food acts "beauty-hindering" in the construction of the human body, and produces symptoms of ugliness and age.

If, according to paradisaic primary laws, the lungs and skin would be given nothing but pure air and sun-electricity, and the stomach and bowels nothing but sun-food, i.e., fruits, which are being digested almost without rest, secreting only mucusless, pasteless and germless cellulose, there seems to be no reason why the tube-system of the human body should become defective, weaken, age and finally break down entirely. Instead of the living energy-cells of the fruit, one eats "killed food," which biologically is meant for beasts of prey, i.e., food chemically changed by air-oxidation (decay), dead-boiled and robbed of its energy. Mucus accumulates especially in the heating channel (stomach and bowels) of the tube-machine, and slowly clogs up the channel and filters (glands). The sum-total of this defilement causes chronic defects, makes one grow old and is the main factor in the nature of all disease. Growing old, therefore, is a latent disease, that is, a slow but constantly increasing disturbance in the operation of the motor of life.

The chemistry of victuals gives the most reliable proof that deformity and decomposition have their source mainly in the lack of minerals in boiled culture-food.

If human ugliness as such, lost beauty and symptoms of growing old can be made accountable for by wrong nourishment, then the theory of beauty and rejuvenation leads to a dietetic cure and a respective improvement of nourishment. But inasmuch as beauty, especially human beauty, cannot be absolutely defined, because everybody has a different taste, I can limit myself only to the main standards of aesthetic demands.

The white corpse-color of the light and sunless man of culture cannot be called beautiful, and emanates mainly from the white corpse-color of the dead-boiled, wrong food. What wonderful color a man can get who feeds on "bleeding" grapes, cherries and oranges and who takes systematically air and sun-baths, cannot be imagined by the modern artists of "pleinair-painting." Mucus and at the same time lack of mineral matter means as much as lack of color. Just compare the food tables of Dr. Konig and you will find that the mucusless food, the fruit and the vegetables, occupy the first place as regards their contents of necessary mineral matter, especially lime. The size of a person, i.e., the circumference of the skeleton, depends for instance, mainly on the amount of lime contained in the food. The Japanese want to increase the size of their race by meat, going thereby from bad to worse. All the pining away of size, deformities of the bones and especially the decay of the teeth, is due to lack of lime. Through the boiling of milk and vegetables in modern cooking the lime is being eliminated. The enormous poorness in mineral of culture-food, especially of the meat as compared with fruit, is responsible for the coming of a toothless human race, as predicted even by physicians, and which is not merely a phantom of imagination. And instead of by fruit these stuffs are being substituted by an organic preparation. The human organism does not assimilate one single atom of mineral substance which has not transmigrated into a plant of fruit, i.e., which has not become organic. The most modern disfigurement, the obesity, has clouded up our aesthetic feeling in this regard so much that we even do not know any longer the limit of the normal. I personally do not even consider the physical culturist "man of muscles of classic type" beautiful and as a standard for the ideal type of Germanic and Aryan races. Weight, shape and especially circumference of body are too great. Every accumulation of fat is pathologic and in this measure unaesthetic. No animal living in freedom is upholstered with fat, like our modern "weight lifters and strong men." The reason is simply too much food and too much fluid; relaxation and clogging of the entire system of vessels are the natural consequences. Grape-sugar of the fruits and their nutritive salts are the right sources for a firm muscle-substance, by which a body disfattened and dis-mucused by fasting can be quickly rebuilt.

The stoutness of face and body are dangerously on the increase; it is ugly and certainly pathologic. It is a curious fact that in our supposedly enlightened age this accumulation of fat is considered not only beautiful, but even a sign of overabundant health, while the daily experience teaches that the slim, permanently youthful type possesses in every respect a greater force of resistance and generally reaches greater longevity.

I should like to be shown just one person of 90 or 100 years with such obesity, which today is pronounced as beautiful and healthy, and with which it is believed to fatten away tuberculosis. If fat people do not die in their best years through palpitation of the heart, apoplexy or dropsy, they succumb to a slow emaciating and the desire for food decreases in spite of all artificial stimulations of the appetite. The skin, especially of the face, having been subjected to extreme tension, becomes foldy and wrinkly. It has lost its youthful elasticity on account of insufficient and unhealthy blood circulation as well as lack of light and sun. And now this relaxation of the skin is being tried to be prevented by salves and powders applied externally! The distinction and beauty of the features, the pureness and healthy color of the complexion, the clearness and natural size of the eyes, the charm of the expression and the color of the lips, age and become ugly to the extent of the expression and color of the mucus in the bowels, which we have recognized above as the central depot from which all the symptoms of diseases, and therefore those of age, are being fed. The "beautiful roundness of cheeks" which at the same time increases the size of the nose, is nothing but a clogging up by mucus, which, as is well known, breaks out in case of a cold in the nose.

The Preservation of the Hair

REASONS FOR BECOMING BALD AND GRAY

I come now to the most important and most striking symptom of the growing-old: the falling out and getting gray of the hair, to which I must devote an entire section, because its appearance generally causes the first and greatest worry and pain over the coming of age, and because hitherto science has stood baffled in the face of this problem.

The modern cutting short of the feminine as well as the masculine hair on the head, and the alarming expansion and earliness of baldness have accustomed even an artistical eye so much to this appearance that we no longer become conscious of the fact of how seriously the aesthetic and harmonic figure of man is disturbed by the voluntary and involuntary "hair-decapitation." Man who is not only intellectual, but also is an aesthetic product of nature, "the crown of creation," is being robbed of the splendid crown of his head—the hair. They could be called "living skulls," these beardless, colorless and expressionless heads of today! Just imagine the most beautiful woman with a pate! Where is the man that would not turn away with horror? Or a fashion-sport of today hewn in marble! In addition to that the mustache shaped geometrically and angular or trimmed off entirely, then the modern clothing which distinguishes itself from that of all the centuries by the greatest insipidity—and this we find beautiful reasons, for which the present-day man gets his beard removed and his hair cut down to a minimum length. The lack of beauty and therewith the unaesthetic appearance of hair and beard has become so general that in course of time the need of shaving and use of the clipper have come as a matter of course. In our time of equalization and all-leveling it is preferred, and rightfully so, to cut off these odor, and so to speak, revelation-organs of inner man, instead of furnishing by ugly, disheveled, uneven and hereditary morbid hair, a living proof for the descendance theory. Therewith we can understand the maltreatment of the hair. The thought has practically given rise that the getting ugly of one organ or of the entire organism means its inner morbidness, i.e., nature reveals internal physiological disturbances of an organism through disharmony of shape and color. The seriously ill and dead organism are its extremes. Doubters of my point of view, and bad nature-observers may here be reminded of the law of exception from the rule, and as regards man—of the fact, that neither hygienically nor aesthetically have we any imagination left of the ideal beauty and health of man living under perfectly natural conditions. If the pleasure in the beautiful is a sentence in the favorable sense, then the displeasure felt by an aesthetic eye in looking upon the disharmony of shape and color must include to a certain degree the recognition of the pathologic.

Let us return to our subject. We know that medical science is powerless as regards baldness, and that cosmetics and chemistry of tonics have failed to produce even a single new hair.

I have already called the hair, especially of the human head, the odor-organs of the body, which are to conduct away the exhalations of the human body. Everybody knows that sweat is produced first of all on the head and in the arm-pits, and that with this sweat, especially on sick people, is connected a disagreeable odor. Dr. Jager calls disease somewhere "stench." This, with exceptions, of course, seems to me correct in so far as I am able to pronounce, on the basis of many years' observation and experiments, the following fundamental uniform conception of disease:

Disease is a fermentation and decay-process of body-substance or of surplus and unnatural food-material which in course of time has accumulated, especially in the digestive organs, and which makes its appearance in the shape of mucus-excretion.

That is, it means in the last instance nothing but the chemical decomposition, the decay of cellular albumen. As is well known, this process is accompanied by stench, while nature combines the originating of new life with fragrance (the building of plants). Properly, man in perfect health should exhale fragrance, particularly so with his hair. Poets are rightfully comparing man with a flower and speak of the hair-fragrance of woman. I, THEREFORE, RECOGNIZE IN THE HAIR OF THE HUMAN A VERY IMPORTANT ORGAN WHICH ASIDE FROM PROTECTIVE AND WARMTH-REGULATING PURPOSES HAS A HIGHLY INTERESTING AND USEFUL DESTINATION: to conduct away the exhalations, the odor of healthy and sick people, which reveals to experts and acute noses not only individual qualities, but even certain disclosures as regards the inner state of health or sickness of a man. If the doctors have not by far recognized digestive disturbances with the microscopes and test glasses, there have yet been certain quacks who have been able to state by simple hair-diagnosis the stench-producing inner process of decay — the disease. Why, there are numberless people today, still youthful and radiating health with a breath like that of a sewer and who are wondering why their hair is falling out.

I have now arrived at the vital spot of my researches and observations.

First one more word about the getting gray of the hair. It has been found that in hair which has become gray the contents of air is increasing, and I am also of the opinion that this "air" consists probably of stinking gases, or at least is mixed with such. I recommend to a chemist with a "strong scent" to discover here the sulphurous acid, then the disappearance of the color of the hair will also have been explained, as it is a well-known fact that sulphur-dioxide bleaches organic substances.

It now seems to me certain, not only theoretically, but also on the basis of my interesting experiments on my own body, that the principal cause of baldness can only be an internal one. If through these odor-tubes or so to speak, "gas chimneys of the head," there must be constantly discharged stinking, corroding gases, very probably impregnated with sulphur-dioxide, instead of natural, fragrant odors, we must not be surprised if the hair together with its roots becomes deathly pale, dies off and falls out. Herewith I claim to have recognized the reason for baldness and to have shown the true way for its cure. I add that about ten years ago, when I was afflicted with chronic inflammation of the kidneys, combined with a high degree of nervosity, my hair had become very gray and fell out. After having been cured from this serious disease by a dietetic treatment I saw that at the same time the gray hairs disappeared and that my hair grew into perfect profusion.

If, therefore, the main cause of baldness lies in the disturbance of digestion and interchange of matter, it can certainly be cured by regulation of these functions. It can be said that even the absolutely bald heads may again take hope, on the basis of my discovery — after all the tonics have failed, and must fail. The reason is that the cause is not external and therefore cannot be got at externally. Whoever sees his hair falling out, or whoever is already bald, and wishes to regenerate in this direction, may apply to me for advice. There is no general internal remedy, and whoever has understood me will appreciate that individualization is necessary in every case. On the basis of the influence of my doctrine of diet on digestion, and creation of clean, pure blood, supplying the correct nourishment of the hair-bed, I can at least guarantee a standstill of the falling out of hair, if my advice is followed correctly.

Thus, all symptoms of ageing are latent disease, accumulation of mucus and clogging-up by mucus. Everybody subjecting himself to a thorough restoring-cure in case of any disease, by parting with the dead cells, through mucusless diet and eventually fasting, rejuvenates himself simultaneously, and whoever submits to a rejuvenating cure, deprives each and every disease of its foundation. Nobody wants to believe in this possibility. Yet, in each scientific dictionary you will find the theory that at the worst one should die only of disturbance in the exchange of matter, i.e., constipation by mucus, so that life ought to end without any disease whatever. This would be the normal; but, alas, the exception — the disease, has become the rule today.

IF ANYBODY WOULD LIVE FROM CHILDHOOD ON ABSOLUTELY MUCUSLESS FOOD, AND FEED ON NOTHING BUT FRUIT, IT WOULD BE JUST AS CERTAIN THAT HE COULD GROW NEITHER OLD NOR SICK. I have seen persons who through a mucusless cure have rejuvenated and become beautiful to such an extent that they could not be recognized. Since thousands of years humanity dreams, imagines and paints the fountain of youth, and looks for it sentimentally to the stars, in the suggestion.

Think of the amounts being expended for remedies for masculine weakness and impotence, for sterility — of course all in vain! And how easy it would be to help some people; especially through correct and nourishing food from the sun-kitchen.

We cannot imagine with what beauty and faculties the paradisiacal "godlike" man was gifted, what wonderful strong, clear voice he had! The beautification and strengthening of the voice, yes, the winning back of the lost voice, is an amazing symptom in my cure, and especially eloquent proof for the really grandiose effect of my system for the entire organism of the patient. I wish to refer here especially to the wonderful success of the cure submitted to by the Royal Bavarian Chamber Singer Heinrich Knote, Munich, under my directions, whose voice had improved to the amazement of the entire musical world.

Increasing Longevity

In the previous chapters I have quoted the clogging-up by mucus as being the reason for disease and ageing. I have also proved the possibility of re-substitution of dead-cells. In view of the latter fact it cannot be denied that the entire standstill of the human motor can be delayed for a long, long time, if the body is being built up and maintained by living sun-food from childhood on. At any rate the body thus nourished is far ahead of that of the wrong food and "all-eater" in that its building material is much more durable. In the right way of living the exchange of matter takes place to a much lesser degree, likewise the stress on the inner organs, especially the heart and the stomach. In the performance of greatest efforts the mucusless organism has not nearly the pulse-frequency of a "much-eater." Merely through this saving of energy it is possible to mathematically figure out and prove an advantage as regards longevity. But can we perhaps even solve by this all-explaining mucus-constipation the last of all mysteries—death?

In life-endangering injuries and afflictions the brain and the heart are the organs whose disturbance of function finally ends with death. We can say that in most diseases death takes place through additional development of heart-illness. As regards this, science has not by far spoken its last word, but we can say that the clogging up of the blood vessels of the heart and the destruction of the tender heart-nerves through permanent re-poisoning of the blood is the final cause of death in all chronic diseases. Likewise the clogging up of the tender blood-vessels in the brain and an eventual bursting of same (apoplexy), as well as any other entire clogging up of vessels to a stand-still of all functions of life produces death. Of course, other circumstances also play a part in it, for instance, insufficient supply of air in case of disease of the lungs. Science also mentions the excessive appearance of the white blood-corpuscles as the reason for death. This process of disease is regarded as a disease in itself, and called "Leukaemia"—white bloodedness, but more proper in my opinion: more mucus than blood. Many other reasons are given for the cause of death.

If, perchance, a disease cannot be put into any of the better defined registers, it is given the name of "cachexy," which sounds very wise but means: bad conditions of nourishment, decay. I now ask, what is really the killing poison? Modern medical science gives the bacilli as the cause for most of the diseases, thus showing that it also has the idea of a common fundamental factor for all diseases, the ageing and death, and undoubtedly a large part of all diseases and their consequences (death) are due to the bacilli. My experimental proof that mucus is the fundamental and main factor differs from the bacillus theory only in that just this mucus is the bed, the pre-condition, the primary.

The excessive appearance of the white blood-corpuscles, i.e., of the white dead mucus, as compared with the red sugar and iron substances, is becoming dangerous to life. Red colored and sweet is the visible token of life and love; white, pale, colorless, bitter; the token of disease and overwhelming by mucus, the slow-dying away of the individual.

The death-struggle or agony can only be regarded as a last crisis, a last effort of the organism to excrete mucus; a last fight of the still living cells against the dead ones and their death-poisons. If the white, dead cells, the mucus in the blood, gain the upper hand, there takes place not only a mechanical clogging-up in the heart, but also a chemical reformation, a decline, a total-poisoning, a sudden decay of the entire blood-supply—and the machine stops short. "It has pleased God Almighty;" "we bend our knees before the mysterious power of death"—thus we speak with resignation.

PART II.
Complete Instructions for Fasting

Most diseases are due to wrong eating habits, incorrect food combinations, acidulous foods and the commercial foods of present day civilization. How to overcome the results of these errors that the majority of us ignorantly inflict upon ourselves will be taught in the following pages.

For thousands of years Fasting has been recognized as Nature's Supreme curative measure. But the art of When, Why and How to fast has been lost by those living in present day civilization with a very few exceptions. The body must have good nourishing food—is the battle cry of today. But just what is good nourishing food?

The unfortunate sufferers go the rounds of the various schools of therapeutics, some of them deliberate fakirs—others unknowingly ignorant but in the majority of cases groping darkly and in vain for the truth. And the unfortunate part of it all is that they die before they learn the truth. Religious evangelists and divine healers have the advantage of giving Nature a chance—prescription "specialists," scientific surgery—serum injectors and vaccine innoculators are the real offenders of an outraged nature. And so it resolves itself into a case of "blind leading the blind." How simple it is to receive instructions from Nature. Watch the animals heal themselves in time of illness—without the use of so-called scientific medicine. This then is the supreme secret of Mother Nature's Self-healing.

In these chapters we intend showing why it is necessary to use cooked foods as well as natural foods to properly balance your diet. We will also explain the causes of fermentation and gas producing foods.

Rational Fasting for Physical, Mental and Spiritual Rejuvenation

It is significant for our time of degeneration that fasting, by which I mean living without solid and liquid food, is still a problem as a leading factor for the average man, as well as for the orthodox medical doctor. Even Naturopathy required a few decades in its development to take up Nature's only, universal and omnipotent "remedy" of healing. It is further significant that fasting is still considered as a "special" kind of cure, and due to some truly "marvelous" results here and there, it has quite recently become a world-wide fad. Some expert Nature-cure advocates plan-out general "prescriptions" of fasting, and how to break a fast regardless of your condition or the cause from which you are a sufferer.

On the other hand, fasting is so feared and misrepresented that the average man actually considers you a fool if you miss a few meals when sick, thinking you will starve to death, when in reality you are being cured. He fails to understand the difference between fasting and starvation. The medical doctor in general endorses and, in fact, teaches such foolish beliefs regarding Nature's only fundamental law of all healing and "curing."

Whatever has been designed and formulated to eliminate the disease matters and designated as "natural treatments" without having at least some restriction or change in diet, or fasting, is a fundamental disregard of the truth concerning the cause of disease.

Have you ever thought what the lack of appetite means when sick? And that animals have no doctors, and no drug stores, and no sanitariums, and no machinery to heal them?

Nature demonstrates and teaches by that example that there is only one disease and that one is caused thru eating—and, therefore, every disease whatsoever it may be named by man, is and can be healed by one "remedy" only—by doing the direct opposite of the cause—by the compensation of the wrong—i.e., reducing the quantity of food or fasting. The reason so many, and especially, long fasting, cures have failed and continue to fail is due to the ignorance which still exists, regarding what is going on in the body during a fast—an ignorance still existing even in the minds of naturopaths and fasting experts up to the present date.

I dare say there may not be another man in history who has studied, investigated, tested and experimented on fasting as much as I did. There is no other expert at present, as far as I know, who conducted so many fasting cures on the most severe cases, as I did. I opened the first special sanitarium in the world for fasting, combined with the Mucusless Diet, and fasting is an essential part of my* Mucusless Diet Healing System. I have likewise made four public scientific tests of fastings of 21, 24 and 32 days, respectively, as a scientific demonstration. The latter test is the **world's record** of a fast conducted under a strict **scientific supervision of government officials.**

You may therefore believe me when I teach something new and instructive about what actually happens in the body during a fast. You have learned that the body must be first considered as a machine, a mechanism made of rubber-like material which has been over-expanded during its entire life thru overeating. Therefore, the functioning of the or-

* Prof. Arnold Ehret is the originator of the Mucusless Diet Healing System. These lessons, now available in book form, are published by Ehret Literature Publishing Co., Beaumont, California 92223.

ganism is continually obstructed by an unnatural over-pressure of the blood and on the tissues. As soon as you stop eating, this over-pressure is rapidly relieved, the avenues of the circulation contract, the blood becomes more concentrated and the superfluous water is eliminated. This goes on for the first few days and you may even feel fine, but then the obstructions of the circulation become greater because the diameter of the avenues become smaller and the blood must circulate thru many parts of the body, especially in the tissues, at and around the symptom, against sticky mucus pressed-out and disolved from the inside walls; in other words, the blood stream must overcome, dissolve and carry with itself mucus and poisons for elimination thru the kidneys.

When you fast you eliminate first and at once the primary obstructions of wrong and too much eating. This results in your feeling relatively good, or possibly even better than when eating, but, as previously explained, you bring new, secondary obstructions from your own waste in the circulation and you feel miserable. You and everyone else blames the lack of food. The next day you can notice with certainty mucus in the urine and when the quantity of waste, taken in the circulation, is eliminated, you will undoubtedly feel fine, even stronger than ever before. So it is a well-known fact that a faster can feel better and is actually stronger on the twentieth day than on the fifth or sixth day—certainly a **tremendous** proof that **vitality does not depend primarily on food,** but rather from an unobstructed circulation. (See Lesson 5 of my Mucusless Diet Healing System.) The smaller the amount of "O" (obstruction) the greater "P" (air pressure) and therefore "V" (vitality).

Thru the above enlightening explanation you see that fasting is—First, a negative proposition to relieve the body from direct obstructions of solid, most unnatural foods; second, that it is a mechanical process of elimination by contracting tissues pressing out mucus, causing friction and obstruction in the circulation.

The following are examples of vitality from "P" Power, air-pressure alone:

One of my first fasters, a relatively healthy vegetarian, walked 45 miles in the mountains on his 24th fast day.

A friend fifteen years younger and myself walked 56 HOURS CONTINUALLY after a ten-day fast.

A German physician, a specialist in fasting-cures, published a pamphlet entitled "Fasting, the Increase of Vitality." He learned the same fact that I did, but he does not know why and how, and vitality therefore remained mysterious for him.

If you drink only water, during a fast, the human mechanism cleanses itself, the same as though you would press out a dirty watery sponge, but the dirt in this instance is sticky mucus and in many cases pus and drugs, which must pass thru the circulation until it is so thoroughly dissolved that it can pass thru the fine structure of the "physiological sieve" called kidneys.

Building a Perfect Body Thru Fasting

As long as the waste is in the circulation you feel miserable during a fast; as soon as it is thru the kidneys you feel fine. Two or three days later and the same process repeats itself. It must now be clear to you why conditions change so often during a fast; it must now be clear to you why it is possible for you to feel unusually better and stronger on the twentieth day than on the fifth, for instance.

But this entire cleasing work, thru continued contracting of the tissue (becoming lean) must be done by, and with the original, old blood composition of the patient, and consequently a long fast, especially a too long fast, may become in fact a crime if the sick organism is too greatly clogged up by waste. Fasters who died from too long a fast did not die from lack of food, but actually suffocated in and with their own waste. I made this statement years ago. More clearly expressed: The immediate cause of death is not a poverty of blood in vital substances, but from too much obstruction. "O" (obstruction) becomes as great as or even greater than "P" (air pressure), and the body mechanism is at its "death point."

I GAVE ALL OF MY FASTERS LEMONADE WITH A TRACE OF HONEY OR BROWN SUGAR FOR LOOSENING AND THINNING THE MUCUS IN THE CIRCULATION. Lemon juice and fruit acids of all kinds neutralize the stickiness of mucus and pus (acid paste cannot be used).

If a patient has ever taken drugs over his entire life period —which are stored up in the body like the waste from food, his condition might easily become serious or even dangerous when these poisons enter the circulation, when he takes his first fast. Palpitation of the heart, headaches, nervousness may set in, and especially insomnia. **I saw patients eliminate drugs they had taken as long as forty years before.** Symptoms such as described above are blamed by everybody and especially doctors on the fast.

HOW LONG SHOULD ONE FAST?

Nature answers this question in the animal kingdom with a certain cruelty — "fast until you are either healed or dead!" In my estimation 50 to 60% of the so-called "healthy" men of today and 80 to 90% of the seriously chronic sick would die from their latent diseases thru a long fast.

How long one should fast cannot be definitely stated at all, in advance, even in cases where the condition of the patient is known. When and how to break the fast is determined by noting carefully **how conditions change during the fast;** — you now understand that the fast should be broken **as soon as you notice that the obstructions are becoming too great** in the circulation, and the blood needs new vital substance to resist and neutralize the poisons.

Change your ideas regarding the claim "the longer you fast the better the cure." You may now readily understand why. Man is the sickest animal on earth; no other animal has violated the laws of eating as much as man; no other animal eats as wrongly as man.

Here is the point where human intelligence can correctively assist in the self-healing process by the following adjustments which embrace the Mucusless Diet Healing System:

First — Prepare for an easier fast by a gradually changing diet toward a mucusless diet, and natural herbal laxatives and enemas.

Second — Change shorter fasts periodically with some eating days of cleansing "mucus-poor" and mucusless diet.

Third — Be particularly careful if the patient used much drugs; especially if a mercury or salpetre, oxide of silver (taken for venereal diseases) have been used, in which case a long, slowly changing, preparative diet is advisable.

An "expert's" suggestion to fast until the tongue is clean caused many troubles with "fanatical" fasters, and I personally know of one death. You may be surprised when I tell you that I had to cure patients from the ill-effects of too long a fast. The reason will be clear later.

In spite of the above, every cure, and especially every cure of diet should start with a two or three-day fast. Every patient can do this without any harm, regardless of how seriously sick he may be. First a laxative and then **an enema daily,** makes it easier as well as harmless.

HOW TO BREAK A FAST

I consider the knowledge of how to break a fast of the utmost importance.

The right food after a fast itself. At the same time, it depends entirely upon the condition of the patient, and very much upon the length of the fast. You may learn from the results of the two extreme cases, both of which ended fatally — not from the fast, but from the first wrong meal — just why this knowledge is so important.

A one-sided meat eater, suffering from diabetes, broke his fast which lasted about a week by eating dates and died from the effects. A man of over 60 years of age fasted twenty-eight days (too long); his first meal of vegetarian foods consisting mainly of boiled potatoes. A necesary operation showed that the potatoes were kept in the contracted intestines by thick, sticky mucus so strong that a piece had to be cut off and the patient died shortly after the operation.

In the first case the terrible poisons loosened in the stomach of this one-sided meat eater during his fast when mixed with the concentrated fruit sugar of the dates, caused at once so great a fermentation with carbonic acid gases and other poisons that the patient could not stand the shock. The correct advice would be: First a laxative, such as a preparation consisting of harmless herbs, later raw and cooked starchless vegetables, a piece of rough bran bread toast. Sauerkraut is to be recommended in such cases. No fruits should be eaten for a long time after the fast has been broken. The patient should have been prepared for the fast by a longer transition diet.

In the second case the patient fasted entirely too long for a man of his age without proper preparation.

Thru these two very instructive examples you may see how individually different the advice must be, and how wrong it is to make up general suggestions concerning how to break a fast.

Important Rules for the Faster

TO BE CAREFULLY STUDIED AND MEMORIZED

What can be said in general, and what I teach is new and different from the average fasting experts, and is as follows:

1 — The first meal and the menus for a few days after a fast must be of a laxative effect, and not of nourishing value as mostly all others think.

2 — The sooner the first meal passes thru the body the more efficiently it carries out the loosened mucus and poisons of the intestines and the stomach.

3 — If no good stool is experienced after two or three hours — help with laxatives and enemas. Whenever I fasted I always experienced a good bowel movement at least one hour after eating, and at once felt fine. After breaking a long fast I spent more time on the toilet than in bed the following night — and that was as it should be.

While sojourning in Italy many years ago, I drank about two quarts of fresh grape juice after a fast. At once, I experienced a watery diarrhea set in foaming mucus. Almost immediately after I experienced a feeling of such unusual strength that I easily performed the knee-bending and arm-stretching exercise 326 times. This removal so thoroughly of obstructions, taking place after a fast of a few days, increased "P" — vitality at once! You will have to experience a similar sensation to believe me, and then you will agree with my formula, "Vitality equals Power minus Obstructions," and you will realize the absurdity of making up scientific nourishing menus for health and efficiency.

4 — The longer the fast the more efficiently the bowels perform after it is over.

5 — The best laxative foods after a fast are fresh sweet fruits; best of all are cherries and grapes, then a little soaked or stewed prunes. These fruits **must not be used after a meateater's first fast,** but only for people who have lived for a certain time on mucusless or at least mucus-poor foods — the "transition diet."

6 — In the average case it is advisable to break the fast with raw and cooked starchless vegetables, stewed spinach has an especially good effect.

7 — If the first meal does not cause any unpleasantness, you may eat as much as you can. Eating only a small quantity of food for the first 2 or 3 days without experiencing a bowel movement — owing to the small amount of food taken — (another wrong advice given by "experts") — is dangerous.

8 — If you are in the proper condition so that you can start eating with fruits, and you have no bowel movement after about an hour, then eat more or eat a vegetable meal as suggested above, eat until you bring out the waste accumulated during the fast with your stool, after eating the first meal.

Rules During the Fast

1 — Clean the lower intestines as well as you can with enemas, at least every other day.

2 — Before starting a longer fast, take a laxative occasionally, and by all means the day before you start the fast.

3 — If possible, **remain in the fresh air,** day and night.

4 — Take a walk, exercise, or some other physical work **only when you feel strong enough to do it;** if tired and weak, rest and sleep as much as you can.

5 — On days when you feel weak, and you will experience such days when the waste is in the circulation, you will find that your sleep is restless and disturbed, and you may

experience bad dreams. This is caused thru the poisons passing thru the brain. Doubt — loss of faith, will arise in your mind; then take this lesson and read it over and over, as well as the other fasting chapters, and especially Lesson 5 of my Mucusless Diet Healing System book. Don't forget that you are, parenthetically speaking, lying on Nature's operating table; the most wonderful of all operations that could be performed; and without the use of a knife! If any extraordinary sensation occurs due to the drugs that are now in circulation, **take an enema at once,** lie down, and if necessary break the fast, **but not with fruits.**

6 — Whenever you arise after lying down, do it slowly; otherwise you may become dizzy. The latter condition is not serious, but you had better avoid it in this manner. It caused me a considerable fear in the beginning, and I know a number of fasters and strict eaters who gave up when they experienced this sensation — lost their faith forever.

FASTING DRINKS

The "fanatic" fasting enthusiast drinks only water. He thinks it best to avoid any trace of food whatever. I CONSIDER A LIGHT LEMONADE WITH A LITTLE HONEY OR BROWN SUGAR OR A LITTLE FRUIT JUICE THE BEST. Drink as often as you care to during the day, but in general, not more than 2 to 3 quarts a day. The less you drink the more aggressive the fast works.

As a change, vegetable juice made from cooked starchless vegetables is very good during a longer fast. Raw tomato juice, etc., is also good. But if fruit juice, for example, orange juice, is used during a longer fast, be extremely careful because the fruit juices may cause the poisons to become loosened too rapidly without causing a bowel movement. I know a number of such fruit and fruit-juice fasts which failed completely because all mucus and all poisons loosened too fast and too much at one time, disturbs all organs too greatly when in the circulation, and have to be eliminated only thru the circulation without the aid of bowel movements.

MORNING FAST OR NON-BREAKFAST PLAN

The worst of all eating habits nowadays is to stuff the stomach with food early in the morning. In European countries, excepting England, no one takes a regular meal for breakfast; it is generally a drink of some kind with bread only.

The only time that man does not eat for 10 or 12 hours is while he is asleep during the night. As soon as his stomach is free from food, the body starts the eliminating process of a fast; therefore encumbered people feel miserable and have a coated tongue upon awakening in the morning. They have no appetite at all, yet they crave food, eat it, and feel better — WHY?

ANOTHER MYSTERY REVEALED

This is one of the greatest problems I solved, and is one that has puzzled all "experts" who believe it is the food itself. As soon as you refill the stomach with food, **THE ELIMINATION IS STOPPED** and you feel better! I must say that this secret which I discovered is undoubtedly the explanation of why eating became a habit and is no longer

—55—

what nature intended it should be, i.e., a satisfaction, a compensation of nature's need of food.

This habit of eating, striking all civilized mankind and now physiologically explained, involves and proves the saying I coined long ago — "Life is a tragedy of nutrition." The more waste that man accumulates, the more he must eat to stop the elimination. I had patients who had to eat several times during the night to be able to sleep again. In other words, they had to put food in the stomach to avoid the digestion of mucus and poisons, accumulated there.

Short Fasts and the Non-Breakfast Plan

During my experience with thousands of fasters I had patients that had to eat several times during the night in order to sleep again. The reason is very apparent. Let me cite an example. Upon awakening you perhaps feel fine — but instead of getting up you remain in bed and fall asleep again — have a bad dream, and actually feel miserable upon awakening the second time. You can understand the exact reason for this.

As soon as you get up, walk around or do something the body is in an entirely different condition than during the sleep. The elimination is slowed down, the energy being used elsewhere.

If eating breakfast is eliminated from your daily menus, you will probably experience some harmless sensation, such as headaches for the first one or two days, but after that you will feel much better, work better, and enjoy your luncheon better than ever. Hundreds of severe cases have been cured by the "non-breakfast-Fast" alone, without important changes in diet; proving that the habit of a full breakfast meal is the worst of all, and most injurious.

It is advisable and really of great advantage to allow the patient to have the same drink for breakfast that he is accustomed to; if he craves coffee, let him continue his drink of coffee, but **absolutely** no SOLID food! Later on, replace the coffee with a warm vegetable juice, and still later change to lemonade. This change should be made gradually for the average mixed eater.

THE 24-HOUR FAST, OR ONE MEAL A DAY PLAN

As with the breakfast-fast you can heal more severe cases with the 24-hour fast, for in cases of deep chronic encumbrance and drugs it is a careful, preliminary step to the necessary longer fasts. The best time to eat is in the afternoon, say, 3 or 4 o'clock P.M.

If the patient is on the mucusless or transition diet, let him eat the fruits first — (fruits should always be eaten first) — and after an elapse of 15 or 20 minutes eat the vegetables; but all should be eaten within an hour so that it is to say, one meal.

FASTING WHEN USED IN CONNECTION WITH THE MUCUSLESS DIET HEALING SYSTEM

As I have stated before, I am no longer in favor of long fasts. In fact it may become criminal to let a patient fast for 30 or 40 days on water — contracting the avenues of circulation — which are continually filling up more and more with mucus, and by dangerous old drugs and poisons, and at the same time rotten blood from his old "stock" — in fact, actually starving from necessary vital food elements. No one can stand a fast of that kind without disadvantage or without harming his vitality.

If fasting is to be used at all, then start at first with the non-breakfast plan; then follow with the 24-hour fast for a while; then gradually increase up to 3, 4 or 5-day fasts, eating between fasts for 1, 2, 3 or 4 days a mucusless diet, combined individually as an elimination adjustment, and at the same time supplying and rebuilding the body continually with and by the best elements contained in and found only in mucusless foods.

Thru such intermittent fasts the blood is gradually improved, regenerated, can more easily tolerate the poisons and waste, and the patient is able at the same time to dissolve and eliminate "disease deposits" from the deepest tissues of the body; deposits that no doctor ever dreamed existed, and that no other method of healing has ever discovered or can remove.

This, then, is the Mucusless Diet Healing System, with fasting an essential part of it.

FASTING IN CASES OF ACUTE DISEASE

"Hunger Cures — Wonder Cures" was the title of the first fasting book I ever read. It gave the experiences of a country doctor, in which he said, "No feverish, acute disease, must nor can end with death if nature's instinctive command, to stop eating thru lack of appetite, is followed."

It is insanity to give food to a pneumonia patient with a high fever, for instance. Having had an unusual contraction of the lung tissues by a "cold" the pressed-out mucus goes into the circulation and produces an unusual heat-fever. The human engine, already thru heat, at the bursting point, becomes more heated thru partaking of solid food, meat broth, etc. (good nourishing foods).

Air-baths taken in the room, enemas, laxatives, cool lemonade would save the lives of thousands of young men who are now daily permitted to die, the innocent victims of pneumonia, or other acute diseases — due to the stubborn ignorance of doctors and so-called highly civilized people.

Fasting for Spiritual Rebirth Thru the Superior Fast

All experts, except myself, believe that you live from your own flesh during a fast. You know now, that what they call metabolism — "metabolize your own flesh when you fast" is simply the elimination of waste.

The Indian "fakir," the greatest fakir in the world today, is nothing but skin and bones. I learned that the cleaner you are, the easier it is to fast, and the longer you can stand it. In other words: In a body free from all waste and poisons, and when no solid foods are taken, the human body functions for the first time in its life without obstructions. The elasticity of the entire tissue system, and of the internal organs, especially of the spongy lungs, work with an entirely different vibration and efficiency than ever before, by air alone and without the slightest obstructions. Stated differently: "V" equals "P" and if you simply supply the "engine" with the necessary water which is used up, you ascend into a higher state of physical, mental and spiritual condition. I call that the "Superior fast."

If your blood "stock" is formed from eating the foods I teach, your brain will function in a manner that will surprise you. Your former life will take on the appearance of a dream, and for the first time in your existence your conscience awakens to a real self-consciousness.

Your mind, your thinking, your ideals, your aspirations and your philosophy change fundamentally in such a way as to beggar description.

Your soul will shout for joy and triumph over all misery of life leaving it all behind you. For the first time, you will feel a vibration of vitality thru your body — like a slight electric current — that shakens you delightfully.

You will learn and realize that fasting and superior fasting (and not volumes of psychology and philosophy) is the real and only key to a superior life; to the revelation of a superior world, and to the spiritual world.

Conclusion

While I have conducted thousands of Fasting cures, any number of people have been helped by simply changing their present dietary habits. The sudden change of diet causes disturbances even in an entirely healthy person. For this reason a change made too rapidly may become dangerous and a complete knowledge is therefore essential.

To relieve and avoid any disturbance of health and at the same time to replace the old tid-bit enjoyments by new and better ones can be accomplished if one follows my transition diet. Changing from meat eating to a strictly vegetarian or fruitarian diet always results in a more vigorous feeling for the first few days; then weakness, great fatigue, possibly headaches and palpitation of the heart set in.

Fruit being the only natural food, loosens and dissolves the mucus, poisons and toxemias and the penned up filth and morass of over-feeding is passed out thru the circulating blood. The dead, decayed tissues are pushed aside to make room for the new living food substances and for the time being the patient loses the change of matter balance. The elimination of poison thru the circulating blood causes more or less disturbance of health. And unless you are thoroughly convinced of the efficacy of the natural diet your friends will dissuade you from further attempts to cleanse the body and will urge an interruption of internal purification in order to save you from what they believe will result seriously and you will soon become lean, the face will appear haggard and drawn and a general depression of feeling may overtake you. This, then, is the healing crisis and if understandingly carried on will result in unhoped for good health. I divide all foods into two kinds.

1. Mucus-forming foods.
2. Non-mucus-forming foods.

Under the first heading we find meat, eggs, fats, milk and all by-products made therefrom, dried beans, dried peas, lentils and ALL STARCHY FOODS.

The second classification embraces: All non-starchy green vegetables and all kinds of fruits. There are certain vegetables and fruits that contain more or less starch and should be given the place of secondary importance in the dietary.

Begin the transition with as much mucus-less foods as possible and as little mucus-forming foods as possible. I call this a mucus-less diet. The next step towards health is the MUCUS-LESS DIET, which means a combination of starchless vegetables and fruits. With the help of this transition diet and some knowledge by the individual to choose and combine rightly, the greatest and most important truth of life is revealed to him. The mis-called strength which we experience after meat-eating is nothing but stimulation, for there is no nourishment for man in meat. Hardening of the arteries, in which fatty, plaque-shaped particles are deposited on the blood vessel walls. They build up a choking lining; in time they may calcify and harden. High-blood pressure often results. This kind of hardening of the arteries is the chief villain in death and disability. Heart attacks, arthritis and diseases of senilty stem from this same cause. The meat-eating animals will die on cooked meats without blood and bones! And rats soon die on an exclusive diet of white flour.

My mucus theory — now a proven fact — has been more and more recognized. It has withstood the test with enormous success and today has a platform that: NATURAL TREATMENT AND DIET IS THE MOST PERFECT AND SUCCESSFUL SYSTEM OF HEALING KNOWN. Thru Rational Fasting and the Mucusless Diet suffering humanity may now have the means of not only relieving but PREVENTING disease, and developing an improved race of people that need never know what diseased conditions are. And my most fervent hope is that it will bring about a better civilized humanity.

— END —

Health and Happiness Through Fasting

by

Fred S. Hirsch

(sketch from original photograph)
Prof. Arnold Ehret
TAKEN AT END OF HIS FORTY-DAY FAST

Health and Happiness Through Fasting
When - Why - Where and How - To Fast

by
Fred S. Hirsch

FASTING requires much more knowledge than the average health seeker considers necessary. Hopefully, this article will help convince you that through fasting lies the road to health and happiness. Few individuals pay much attention to the underlying causes of human illness, or the vital problems of what food is best for human consumption, and as a result we innocently contribute to our own miseries and ailments through over-indulgence in eating incompatible food combinations, excessive worry, tension and over-work. Meat, alcoholic stimulants, dairy products and starchy foods are all contributing factors.

FASTING must first be recognized as Nature's way of healing all ills, and while not a "cure-all" for every known ailment, total fasting makes it possible for Nature in her desperate and continuous effort to remove and expel the foreign matter and disease producing toxemic wastes from the body, thereby correcting the faults of wrong living and improper diet.

FASTING may not be adapted to everyone, under every condition, but fortunately, fasting can prove acceptable to the great majority. Nature alone possesses the true healing power and our body can therefore be designated a "self-curative" organism. For centuries past we have been taught to look upon illness, "disease", as some deliberate affliction visited upon us whether deserved or not — whereas in truth it is actually Nature's "house-cleaning" effort! When this truism finally becomes recognized, and Nature, the great healer is permitted to carry on, you will note a vast improvement in your health. Suppressing ailments and symptoms of pain through use of sedative and pain relieving drugs must eventually result in the illness becoming chronic. During the course of a life time toxemic wastes are continually being discharged and it is claimed that the body and all vital organs have been renewed many times. Correcting wrong dietetic habits will permit the body to take advantage of this natural phenomenon and build clean healthy tissue! Only through a total fast can this be satisfactorily brought about. Voluntary abstinence from food for restoring normal bodily vigor was instinctive with primitive man. Start fasting one or two days, drinking water only, to which a few drops of lemon or lime juice has been added, especially if distilled water is used. At about four or five o'clock in the afternoon, break the fast with a light laxative or enema. You will be shocked at the amount of waste that is now being thrown off almost immediately. This mass of previously uneliminated waste was poisoning your blood stream circulation continuously. This should help convince you that here is the way — and the only way, to health!

It is the height of folly to expect modern "miracle drugs" to do more than to temporarily suppress the aches and pains of "disease". Because of the sedative ability of the narcotic drug to deaden the inflamed nerves and tissues for a few hours at most, Nature's "warning signals" are thereby ruthlessly disregarded! Arnold Ehret truthfully claims that "the basic cause of all latent disease of man, whatever its official name may be, is a clogged up tissue system of uneliminated, unused and undigested food substances. Disease is still a mystery to every Doctor who fails, or deliberately refuses, to understand and recognize these simple facts!" Disease consists of a "foreign matter" which has weight, and which must be eliminated from the body before the patient can hope to get well. Every sick person must, therefore, go through the healing process of a "cleansing" so that the body may have the opportunity of eliminating the sticky "mucus", which has been stored in the tissues or held in the pockets of the intestines for years and which interfere with the proper digestive and blood-building functions. Unfortunately, fasting is so feared by the average individual that he actually believes starvation will result thru missing a few meals — when in reality he is being helped, and many practitioners fail to grasp, or fully understand, that there is a vast difference existing between fasting and starvation. A sure proof of the efficacy of fasting is to discontinue all food intake, with the exception of water, for a day or two. Note how the tongue (being an organ of elimination) becomes thickly coated with mucus. The odor of decaying foods is on your breath and the bowel eliminations become offensive. Probably for the first time the body has now been given an opportunity of eliminating the over-abundance of stored up wastes and encumbrances clogging up the tissues! Having assured yourself of the desirability of ridding your body of unwanted waste and encumbrances, the remedy consists of a series of short fasts — each fast to be followed by a "cleansing diet" of fruits and green leaf vegetables, eaten either in their natural or cooked state. This "cleansing program" must be continued just so long as complete recovery to normal health is absent.

How Long Should One Fast

Every person has an individual problem — age of patient, nature of the illness, amount and type of drugs previously used. In fact, so many considerations need be given full recognition of this subject that the list would be endless. Fasting is Nature's oldest, yet least expensive, and in our opinion, best method of treating disease. In fact, fasting can be considered the cornerstone of Natural Healing, and its value without equal. How long should one fast becomes important since long fasts of thirty to fifty days could become dangerous unless properly conducted and supervised by a knowledgeable authority. It is, therefore, wisest for the faster to adopt a series of short fasts, i.e.: two or three days of each week, gradually increasing the length of each succeeding fast, a day or more if necessary, but not to exceed more than a week of total fast at one time. This will enable the chronically ill body to gradually and slowly eliminate these toxic waste materials responsible for their illness without seriously affecting normal body functioning, after which a corrected mode of living will restore the individual to a virile, vigorous state of health. Fasting for overcoming both acute and chronic ailments is centuries old — dating back to the beginning of life itself. No claim is made that fasting is necessarily a pleasant experience, yet the faster often receives blessed relief from physical pain, plus self-satisfaction, in the knowledge that the fast might eventually result in complete cessation of all pain and, hopefully, a return to normalcy! Primarily, a fast is undertaken for a good reason — the individual is desirous of correcting and overcoming illness, or a depleted loss of vital power which has already manifested itself threatens to become chronic — so the answer to "how long should one fast", becomes clear — i.e.: continue the short fasts until the illness has been overcome and disease no longer exists! This suggestion, of course, refers directly to the length of time that the series of "shorter fasts", as previously outlined, are to be continued.

Why to Fast

The search for health goes on unceasingly and while fasting has helped untold thousands of sufferers to regain normal health it is essential that we must know when, how and why to fast in order that we might receive the greater amount of physical and mental benefit.

Arnold Ehret in his "Mucusless Diet Healing System" tells us: "Every disease, no matter what name it may be known by in medical science, is CONSTIPATION — a clogging up of the entire pipe system of the human body." Please note that Ehret uses the word "constipation" to apply to "a clogging up (a constipation) of the entire human pipe system" and not merely a "bowel evacuation", the ordinarily accepted usage of the word. He refers specifically to the accumulation of waste toxic matters in the tissues and in the blood stream, the lungs, kidneys, bladder, stomach, intestinal tract — in fact, every organ of the entire body. And since in Ehret's opinion 99-9/10% of all ailments directly result from the same causes, he aptly refers to all common ailments as "the oneness of disease." Hence, the method of correction of the common cold, bronchitis, asthma, sinusitis or tuberculosis, can best be accomplished through fasting since in his opinion all ailments are the direct result of a "clogged up" overloaded mucus condition brought about through wrong dietetic habits — i.e.: the over-eating of "mucus-forming" types of food.

The simple remedial expedient is to discontinue doing that which was the original cause of the condition. Fast, and thereby give Nature an opportunity to eliminate these "toxic waste matters" which Ehret calls "mucus". High blood pressure, migraine or other types of headches, cardiac conditions or peptic ulcers, colitis, rickets, anemia, neuritis or acidosis, epilepsy, glaucoma, urinary disturbances of the bladder, nephritis, tumors, or even sterility, to name but just a few, according to Ehret's teachings, consists of an overloaded mucus condition existing throughout the entire body, directly traceable to the one great dietic sin — gluttonous over-eating of incorrect food mixtures. Ehret's claim that 99-9/10% of all ailments actually result from the one cause, wrong food combinations and "gluttony"; remains unshaken! Forcing ourselves to eat when no appetite exists because of the prevalent and popular belief that we must eat to gain strength and vitality, can result in the temporary loss of all desire for food of any kind and, unfortunately, the results of this forced eating of — "plenty of good nourishing foods" may actually produce an entirely opposite result! We end up building disease rather than gaining vitality — and ofttimes permanent illness is the net result! All of which teaches us that strength, vitality and good health are by no means dependent upon the *quantity* of our food intake but rather through the actual amount of properly digested and assimilated food eaten that can be used by the body.

Fasting can start you on the road to the fulfillment of an enjoyable, pleasant, happy way of life; and the end result of following a natural method of eating and living is a longer, healthful life! These are but a few reasons "why to fast".

When and How to Fast

Dr. Frank McCoy, in his book, "The Fast Way to Health", recounts hundreds of cases who were greatly helped through an exclusive liquid diet consisting of nothing but fresh orange juice. The patient reported to Dr. McCoy's office daily, for periods of three to six weeks. Besides the orange juice diet other modalities, such as massage, vibrating machines, colonic irrigations and Chiropractic adjustments, were also used in the treatment to keep the patient occupied, and Dr. McCoy gives all credit to the fast. Bernarr McFadden, the well-known Physical Culturist, received much publicity through advocating an exclusive milk diet and thousands of persons claim to have received great benefit from the McFadden milk diet. Both the fresh orange juice, and milk diet, properly should come under the category of what could be called a "camouflaged fast". In other words, the body is permitted to "rest" and rebuild since the one type of food only, requires considerably less vitality to digest. The over-worked organs are thus given an opportunity to slow down, permitting the rebuilding of the patient's vitality. Unused morbid waste encumbrances are eliminated and the previously overworked body can now carry on the normal digestive process. An exclusive "milk diet" can cause constipation and for this reason has proven undesirable. On the other hand Dr. McCoy's fresh orange juice diet, when used by a patient heavily encumbered with concentrated poisons, might cause too rapid an elimination of these concentrated poisons to be released into the blood stream, and it might even be conceivable, in fact; without proper supervision this condition could end disastrously.

To attempt a long fast, and at the same time continue to carry on our daily chores or work as usual, is not entirely fair to the faster since, after all, we must not overlook the fact that during the fast we are actually on "Nature's operating table". A considerable amount of bodily vitality is consumed during the process of throwing off these age-old "poisons and toxic waste materials", and justifiably a complete rest — even to the point of remaining in bed during the entire period of the fast, is often indicated. In other words, a complete physical rest and mental relaxation should be the rule if at all posible during such strenuous "house-cleansing" periods. The form of fasting known as a liquid diet, especially if the liquids consist of fresh vegetable juices or cooked vegetable broth (celery, carrots, parsley, onions, tomatoes, etc.) or, fruit juices, can be continued up to sixty days or more without overtaxing the patient's vital forces. But when fresh grapes, orange or grapefruit juice is used exclusively considerably more caution must be the rule since these particular juices have a decidedly potent ability to "stir-up" toxic wastes rapidly. Thrown into the blood circulation too rapidly, especially after a long total fast when the poisons being eliminated are in a concentrated form, the blood stream becomes over loaded with these poisonous waste materials and normal body functioning is seriously disarranged. Dizzy spells often occur, followed by severe diarrhea and vomiting — and while this might be only a temporary condition it requires careful observation and attention. Should this physical reaction persist it is, of course, advisable, and imperative, to discontinue the fast immediately, especially the use of all fresh fruits, and return to eating only cooked vegetables containing much roughage, i.e.: spinach, beets, sauerkraut, etc., or even meats (particularly if the patient has been a one-sided meat eater) temporarily, at least until the body functioning returns to normal and all symptoms of dizziness have completely disappeared. All types of fruits and vegetables, including the fresh frozen fruits and vegetables, are much less "aggressive" as far as their eliminating ability is concerned, when cooked or baked. Now you may appreciate why it is so necessary that you take into consideration the amount of existing waste and "poisonous" toxic matters in your body before undertaking a long fast. Even the innocent appearing "soothing syrups" given to infants contain some form of "narcotics" in minute dosage — hence, the extreme importance of having complete knowledge beforehand in more ways than one!

We need only to look to the animal world to learn the importance that wise Mother Nature places in fasting. All sick, seriously ill, or wounded animals immediately discontinue eating food and go on a total fast in a secluded place where they can relax from all activity until they have completely regained their health and vigor. This could require a period of time as long as a week, or a month, but their patience is always rewarded with success. Complete fasting without food or water of a number of animals during their long winter hibernation is a well known phenomenon, and it is even customary for many animals to fast during the "nursing period", remaining with their young until weaned. Fasting must be recognized as a natural and safe method of care of the sick body, a method by which the person is enabled to overcome illness through eliminating, almost miraculously, the cause of the ailment, and yet it can be said there is nothing "miraculous" about it! Whether we fast to restore health, gain or lose weight, or merely to retain our present bodily vigor, we soon recognize that fasting is a vital factor through which we may increase our vitality and personal well-being, both mentally and physically. Besides readily overcoming such minor discomforts as the common cold or indigestion, fasting, undoubtedly, adds to your life span! The digestive process uses up precious vitality — contrariwise, fasting has been known to actually rebuild vital forces, and the conclusion must become self-evident that fasting prolongs life itself! It is necessary, therefore, that we repeat over and over again the importance of entering upon a fast intelligently, confident in the final outcome, with complete understanding and knowledge, and we specifically refer to the longer fasts of thirty to sixty days duration. It is essential, for example, that the faster knows the difference between "false" and "real" appetite. Hunger pangs caused through "false appetite" can generate rather severe pains in the stomach region, together with various emotional disturbances and a corresponding feeling of weakness. Since the eating of food will at this period immediately cause stoppage of the distress symptoms it is only natural for the faster to surmise that lack of food was the cause, and eating; the remedy, whereas the opposite might be true. Our established life-long habit of eating "by the clock" has firmly affixed in our minds the desirability of eating at that precise time. The fact of the matter is that true hunger can only take place when a real need for food exists! The individual who is always hungry is, in fact, "pathologically unwell". Surely no need for food exists when hunger is lacking. Never force yourself to eat unless you are *truly* hungry and a keen relish for food exists. Otherwise, you merely add work to an already "overworked" digestive tract. All excess food becomes a burden and this, of course, is especially true in cases of illness. Over-eating, or forced feeding, retards recovery by requiring the body to use its precious vitality in the elimination of this un-needed food. Often this "good nourishing" diet is actually to blame for the patient's loss of weight and lessened vitality! Even in the healthy body, when over-eating or gluttony is indulged in, it can cause vomiting and diarrhea, for the healthy organ rejects all excess food. Contrariwise, when the quantity of food intake is decreased (lessened) bodily energy is conserved since the digestive organs have less work to do — liver, pancreas, heart and arteries are relieved of a greater portion of their labor, all of which, naturally, results in an increase of the healing process! Witholding all food intake from the sick patient causes every depurating organ in the entire body to increase its eliminating activity, It starts immediately to get rid of all poisonous wastes and a cleansing of the entire tissue system begins. Nothing equals the fast as a means of eliminating age-old stored up wastes from an over-loaded tissue system. Nature's constant and unceasing effort, therefore, is to remove all unusable and excess waste substances from the body and fortunately for us this constant elimination goes on continuously if good health is to be the result. To be willing to settle for half health, or less, when real health is possible is to rob yourself of life's most precious possession. Aristotle, that great Greek philosopher, said over 2300 years ago — "If there is one way better than another, it is the way of Nature". Much vital energy is required during this cleansing process, but paradoxical as it might seem, the faster usually gains both in strength and weight. The feverish patient already lacks the necessary vitality to digest food while suffering pain yet "nourishing food" continues to be advised. Unfortunately, the popular idea that man must eat every few hours in order to stay alive remains; despite the fact that it has been proven over and over again that the "sick person"actually gains in strength when food is withheld and suffers a relapse from forced feeding! How many thousands of patients have been innocently "fed" into premature graves through ignorance of Nature's laws? No claim is herein made that fasting alone, regardless of the advanced stage of the illness, or bodily and mental condition of the patient will produce the sure cure. Common sense and caution must be your guide during the fast and we can safely predict that in the majority of cases the faster will become physically stronger and more vital and mentally alert — up to the point, of course, that the individual is capable of accepting. Unfortunately, fasting, when used in far advanced cases as a last resort, or in long standing chronic cases, especially in the elderly person of lowered vitality, cannot be expected to produce the 'miracle". Terminal cases, for example, can only hope for a lessening of the discomfort of their pain. Total fasting is not indicated in these terminal cases but worthwhile results, merely through reducing the quantity of food intake, are often experienced. An extremely limited, carefully selected, diet in all cases should be carried on — and, remember, over-feeding can only result in increased suffering. Dr. J. H. Tilden, M.D., conducted thousands of fasts in his Denver Sanitarium and authored many books on the subject of fasting. He wrote, "I must say in all seriousness that fasting when combined with a properly selected diet is the nearest approach to a 'cure-all' that is possible to conceive — profoundly simple and simply profound!"

Without exception, all of the modern "miracle drugs", including Aspirin drugs employed today to restore the sick and ailing to normal health, have been known to result in great bodily harm. It is well known, and readily acknowledged, that they act as a palliative and not a cure, yet often the ill effects they cause are not discovered until many years after taking, before reactions occur in the affected organ and are recognized. When the cause of illness is finally removed and the restorative process of true healing is given the opportunity to function Nature's remarkable "rebuilding" process takes place and proceeds in an orderly manner in accordance with Natural Physiological Law! Wounds are healed, broken bones are mended, destroyed tissues are replaced, and we can positively state that these healing processes have never been duplicated through any method or laboratory finding as yet devised by mere man! It is true that the scientist has kept living tissue alive and growing in his laboratory, but he has never been able to reproduce living tissue, nor has he developed a man-made substitute for the natural life process through which healing is accomplished! Nature's healing process starts instantly when the need occurs, and we must recognize the importance of aiding Nature through fasting, since we now know that the healing process increases when the body is freed from disposing of surplus food. Only a total abstinence from food makes it possible for the sick body to function thoroughly, in its own inimitable way, during the healing period. As previously mentioned, Arnold Ehret preferred the so-called "short fast" of three days to a week or ten days for the average individual. It was his experience that satisfactory results could be obtained through a series of so-called "shorter" fasts, especially in cases where the patient is not under competent supervision and "on his own" so to speak. It is well for the individual to decide on how long he intends to carry on before initiating the fast. Let us say, for example, that the patient is of the "nervous", high-strung or imaginative type, or he may even be skeptical of results that might occur. He must first of all create an enthusiastic desire to fast. If the slightest doubt of final success is permitted to enter his mind then not more than two or three days should be the extent of the fast in this case. Hopefully, the resulting good feeling will quiet all future unnecessary fears, and the next fast can be for a longer period, even up to a full week.

The over-weight individual finds it much easier to go without food. Loss of weight causes no fear, and the patient's mental attitude makes fasting almost a pleasure! A week, or perhaps ten days for this type of individual, brings practically no discomfort whatsoever. The first day's hunger pangs perhaps are the most difficult. A mouthful of water (held for ten or fifteen minutes before expectorating) will lessen the "false appetite" craving for food, which decreases as the fast progresses. The seriously sick, or severely injured individual, has absolutely no desire for food, so fasting comes naturally. A safe rule to follow is to stop eating until appetite has returned, or until you feel completely well.

When to Fast

Nature has selected the spring of the year for the annual "house-cleaning" period. The very types of the first green leaf vegetables and fruits that Nature brings forth and amply supplies in the early spring give significant testimony to this fact. The green leaf vegetables and herbs are proven blood purifiers, well known over the centuries, and because of their laxative qualities they are recognized efficient "cleansers".

This same description applies as well to the first fruits of the season. Cherries, for example, one of the earlier fruits to ripen, have long been recognized for their "cleansing" ability. Their enticing color appeal, plus the sweet and delicious flavor, particularly when gathered and eaten direct from the tree, will produce remarkable blood purifying and "cleansing" results. An exclusive cherry diet for five or six days is a "camouflaged fast" well worth trying. Since the body's resistance to cold weather is lowered during the fast it is more pleasant to fast during the warmer weather, but this is not to say that we should wait until warm weather returns before undertaking a fast if the need for fasting exists. Postponing the fast, awaiting warmer weather could prove inadvisable for a delay might conceivably result in the ailment becoming more involved. It is very easy for the patient to remain indoors while fasting and remain comfortable during the coldest weather.

Why to Fast

Fasting is indicated in many instances. At the first indication of the "common cold" for example, fasting becomes a preventative measure! Start the "cleansing" (fasting) program before a more serious, chronic condition develops! Minor ailments such as headaches, biliousness, nervousness, injuries and even excessive grief, all indicate the desirability of missing a meal or two. The length of time must, of course, depend entirely on the condition of the faster. For more serious ailments, the amount of toxic waste and foreign encumbrances present in the blood stream must be taken into consideration and often a longer fast is indicated. Age of the faster is another important factor since we cannot expect to overcome the effects of a life time of wrong living within a few short days, or weeks. The chronic sufferer, therefore, must exercise patience and perseverance in his efforts to return to normal health. It is to be expected that in many instances the faster becomes discouraged, even frightened, at the actual results that the fast brings about during the early stages of the "house-cleansing" period. But with complete faith and knowledge of what is actually occurring the final results will eventually prove very worthwhile. A little "self-discipline" would provide many of us with a steady flow of energy and a wonderful sense of inner well being that comes from a healthy body.

Where to Fast

Often times where to fast must be given a great deal of consideration. The inevitable opposition of the well-meaning members of the "family" often proves to be the most difficult of the obstacles to overcome. Our loved ones, because of the inborn fear of starvation inculcated in all of us since early childhood, find it impossible to withhold well intentioned warnings and often plead tearfully with the faster to "eat something". They honestly and sincerely believe that great bodily harm, even death itself, will inevitably result from a fast of more than a few days at most! Their pleadings when ignored often lead to hysterical and angry efforts to force the faster to "eat some good nourishing food" and the unfortunate sick person, already weakened through illness, loses his original determination to "get well or else" — and succumbs to their pleadings by "eating something" which often are the very foods that should not be used! It may well be that the faster himself is not completely "sold" to the efficacy of the fast — in which case he can be more easily swayed from his original plan to continue the fast, since he lacks the courage of his own convictions. Should this experience be yours, then at least eat the foods that you know are indicated for breaking the fast, as taught by Prof. Arnold Ehret, in order to accomplish the most good. It might be wise under these conditions to arrange for suitable supervision at a sanitarium or rest home specializing in fasting, particularly if the faster contemplates a longer fast of two or three weeks duration. Never lose sight of the fact that the faster is on "Nature's 'bloodless' operating table" and should, therefore, be made comfortable at all times through adequate nursing care, daily sponge baths, massage, colonic irrigations, with complete rest and relaxation, so that the bodily strength and comfort can be retained and even increased. To obey Nature's laws means health—to disregard, whether through ignorance or deliberately, means pain, disease and even death. In other words, health is not merely an accident but an achievement—for the orderly working of the body functions spells HEALTH and its derangement results in disease. The warning signs of pain and discomfort signify that Nature's laws have been digressed, whether unintentionally or not! Freedom from pain, or HEALTH, means that they have been complied with. In the overwhelming majority of illness, all that Nature requires for health to be gained in a discontinuance from doing that which was the original cause of the disease—yet our natural instinct to fast, even missing a single meal, has become lost through present day "civilization" and the increase in all human ills can be directly traced to the accepted customs of our advanced "civilization".

How Long to Fast

The exact length of the fast need not be *definitely* decided beforehand. The various physical and mental reactions which take place during the fast could understandably often cause needless alarm both to the faster and the inexperienced physician. For the first time in years, possibly for the first time in the life of the faster, a thorough cleansing of the tissue system is possible and stored up toxemic wastes and poisons are now being carried off as the avenues of circulation contract permitting the existing over-pressure to be rapidly relieved. Renewed vitality enables the blood stream to discharge the dissolved mucus and toxemic waste materials now in circulation for elimination, and these "poisonous encumbrances" might cause a feeling of being "ill" to exist during this period. You will find, however, that just as soon as the "cleansing process" is completed and the wastes are eliminated, the faster feels stronger than ever before! Ehret often remarked about his fasting patients actually feeling stronger on the third week of the fast than they did during the first week! The unobstructed blood circulation can now produce increased vitality — further proof that Nature heals through fasting. It is this elimination of waste, poisonous materials with which the tissues and intestinal tract have been "clogged up" for years, and now finally removed, that make it possible for normal bodily function to once again take place. It is Nature alone, in the final analysis, through fasting and the resulting elimination of waste materials through the various depurating organs, i.e.: the skin, kidneys, lungs, bowels, as well as our eyes, ears and nose, that aid the true healing process to take place. "The mills of the Gods grind slowly yet they grind exceedingly fine!"

In the final summation we cannot emphasize too strongly the fact that what we know as disease is in reality a "process of purification" — a special effort as it were, on the part of the abused, sick organism to throw off the abnormal quantities of latent poisonous waste materials. Our perverted dietetic habits, the result of false teachings since childhood, are the origin. We attempt to "stop" the pain through unnatural means rather than recognize pain as Nature's warning signal of a local symptom of a general disorder. The majority of persons, never having experienced the feeling of real health and vitality, are not cognizant of what they are missing. They little suspect that mankind's greatest enemies — ignorance, selfishness, greed and gluttony, the cause of all his physical and mental woes exist within himself! Discontinue careless and indulgent over-eating! Comply with Nature's unchangeable laws for safe guidance in your search for health! Fasting gives the body an opportunity to correct these faults of improper dieting — and incompatible food combinations. To enjoy this more abundant, healthier life is within your reach. The sooner you make the decision to start the better off you surely will be. Why not grasp this opportunity and let us help you attain your desired goal of a longer, happier, healthier, more vigorous life.

Become a disciple of health, and prove to yourself that strict, self-discipline brings worthwhile results. Then, thru precept and example, hold high the torch of knowledge and enlightenment to your fellow-man, who while teetering on the very brink of physical and mental collapse finds himself still unable to grasp these simple truths, nor understand the cause of his suffering. Make him anxious to travel the broad road to health leading to a completely new — wonderful, joyous life of physical, spiritual and mental regeneration.

FINIS

Other Publications by Arnold Ehret

MUCUSLESS DIET HEALING SYSTEM —
13th Edition   24 Lessons   194 pages.

A complete usable program by Arnold Ehret. Explains in plain, easily understood language the Ehret teachings. $2.95

DEFINITE CURE OF CHRONIC CONSTIPATION.
6th Edition

A comprehensive statement of causes of Constipation, and how they may be avoided. Also article on "Overcoming Constipation Naturally." $1.00

PHYSICAL FITNESS THRU A SUPERIOR DIET.

Also A Religious Concept of Physical, Spiritual and Mental Dietetics. Building a Perfect body thru Fasting and Dietetics. The Author proves that a high degree of civilization can be developed in relation to health. Revised edition. $1.00

THUS SPEAKETH THE STOMACH also THE TRAGEDY OF NUTRITION. 5th Edition. A novel approach in which Prof. Ehret, lets the stomach, the germinating center of all diseases, tell the story of the tragedy of man's nutrition. $1.00

ROADS TO HEALTH & HAPPINESS. Contains Your Road to Regeneration by Arnold Ehret.
My Road to Health by Teresa Mitchell.
Build your own Road to Health by Teresa Mitchell.
Internal Uncleanliness—by Fred S. Hirsch—all based on the Ehret teachings. $1.00

EHRET LITERATURE PUBLISHING CO.
BEAUMONT, CALIFORNIA 92223